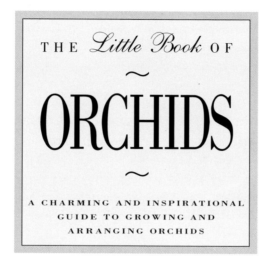

THE *Little Book* OF

~

ORCHIDS

~

A CHARMING AND INSPIRATIONAL
GUIDE TO GROWING AND
ARRANGING ORCHIDS

Editor: Jo Finnis

Contributor: Janice Seymour p.50-9

Designer: Sally Strugnell

Original Design Concept: Peter Bridgewater, Nigel Duffield

Picture Researchers: Miriam Sharland, Leora Kahn

Director of Production: Gerald Hughes

Typesetting: Julie Smith

Photography: MARY EVANS PICTURE LIBRARY p.8, 9. BRIDGEMAN ART LIBRARY, London, with
acknowledgments to: Christie's London, for A Bazaar in Constantinople/J Brindesi, p.10-11;
the V & A Museum, London, for Purple Orchis and Primrose/Thomas F Collier, p.15. ART RESOURCE,
NewYork: p.36-7. Natural Science Photos: jacket flap; Tim Oliver, p.16-17, 60; Dick Scott, p.22-3;
J Hobday, p.24-5, 44-5; F N Gandon, p.27. NATIONAL TRUST PHOTOGRAPHIC LIBRARY,
© National Trust 1992: Jonathan Plant, p.19. Eric Crichton: p.38-9. Boys Syndication: p.42-3.
All other photographs by Neil Sutherland © CLB Publishing.

MALLARD PRESS

An imprint of BDD Promotional Book Company Inc., 666 Fifth Avenue, New York, N.Y. 10103.

Mallard Press and the accompanying duck logo are registered trademarks of the
BDD Promotional Book Company, Inc, registered in the U.S. Patent and Trademark Office. Copyright © 1992.

CLB 3130 © 1992 Colour Library Books Ltd, Godalming, Surrey, England.

First published in the United States of America in 1992 by the Mallard Press.

Printed and bound in Singapore.

ISBN 0-7924-5811-7

THE *Little Book* OF
ORCHIDS

DAVID SQUIRE

MALLARD
PRESS

Below: *The roots of orchids resemble testicles and for this reason they were crushed and eaten to encourage sexual activity.*

Medicinal Roots

Nearly 3,000 years ago the Chinese are said to have written about orchids, but the earliest reference in western civilization is by the Greek writer and botanist, Theophrastus. He mentions orchids in his *Enquiry into Plants*, written three centuries before the birth of Christ.

Orchids became part of early medicine at a time when the treatment of an illness was frequently based on the assumption that human ailments were best cured by parts of plants that resembled the areas being treated. The roots of orchids, considered to resemble testicles, were crushed and eaten in an attempt to encourage sexual activity, a practice that continued until the seventeenth century. The roots of orchids were also used to cure King's-evil, a condition characterized by running neck sores.

Right: *In the seventeenth century, orchids were used in several medicinal preparations, sold through grocer and druggist shops.*

Culinary Delicacy

Nicholas Culpeper mentions 'salep' as a food derived from the bases of orchids that gives support during famine, but it has a much longer history. The nutritious starch-like substance known as 'bassorin' has a sweetish taste and was used instead of starch as a preservative. In Turkey and Iran it has been used for many centuries and exported as 'sahlep', anglicized as 'salep' and 'saloop'. Long before coffee was introduced from Arabia - first to Constantinople, later to Central Europe and in 1650 to England - this starch-like material was used to create a nutritious drink. Until the early 1900s it was still sold in the streets of Istanbul as a hot winter drink. Indeed, the English essayist Charles Lamb during the early 1800s talks of a salopian shop in Fleet Street, London.

Left: *Salep, a nutritious hot winter drink made from orchids, was sold in the streets of Istanbul until the early 1900s.*

11

Confectioner's Delight

At one time, the orchid *Vanilla planifolia* was the main source of vanilla and widely used to flavor chocolate and other sweets. An alternative but inferior source of vanilla was the West Indian vanilla *(Vanilla pompona)*.

Native to Mexico, *Vanilla planifolia* produces beans (pods) that, when dried and cured, produce vanillin, the active principle of vanilla. Incidentally, the Aztecs in South America used this plant as a flavoring long before Christopher Columbus set sail from Europe in 1492.

Vanillin is now produced synthetically, but when obtained from this orchid the pods were cured by dipping them in almost boiling water for 25 seconds. They were then alternately placed between blankets to 'sweat' and in the sun to dry. They were then rolled in a blanket and placed in a closed box, being taken out each day and spread in the sun for one or two hours. This process was continued for two to three weeks until the pods became brown and pliable.

Above: *William Shakespeare made reference to 'long purples' – Early Purple Orchids – in* Hamlet.

Love Potions

The Early Purple Orchid *(Orchis mascula)*, also known as the Blue Butcher, differs from most terrestrial orchids in having tubers slightly resembling two or three finger-like lobes. For this reason, it has been known as Dead Men's Fingers. In William Shakespeare's *Hamlet* there is a reference to this orchid:

'There with fantastic garlands did she come,
Of crow-flowers, nettles, daisies, and long purples,
But our cold maids do dead men's fingers call
them:'

A love potion derived from the Early Purple Orchid is said to have been created by squeezing out the nectar from 20 stems into warm goat's milk or Greek yogurt. John Partridge, physician to Charles I of England, suggested it *'have great force to provide the desire for coition and doth egregiously excite both sexes therewith'*.

Witches are said to have used the tubers of orchids in love charms, also known as philtres.

14

Above: *The Early Purple Orchid* (Orchis mascula)
*is a common European orchid, growing in open
woodland, often alongside bluebells and primroses.*

Orchid Language

Conveying a message in a subtle way without *'inking the fingers'* was known in Constantinople, now Istanbul, in the 1600s. Flowers were associated with sentiments that mostly had amorous overtones.

It was not only the flower itself that carried a meaning but its positioning as well. Turned to the left, the flower would convey one meaning, while the opposite inclination would imply a different thought. The hand that offered the flower also contributed to the sentiment.

Confusingly, some flowers have several meanings, depending on how they are spelt. For instance, the Bee Orchid *(Ophrys apifera)* means

Left: *The Bee Orchid* (Ophrys apifera) *signifies 'industry' in the language of flowers.*

'industry', but when spelt Bee Ophrys - clearly still the Bee Orchid - means 'error'. Confusion arises from the use of common names and both current and old botanical names at the same time. The genus Ophrys is only one of the many genera within the orchid family.

The orchid known in flower language as the Butterfly Orchis, now the Butterfly Orchid, signifies 'gaiety'. The confusion between Orchis and Orchid arises from the fact that at one time this orchid was in the genus *Orchis*. The Spider Ophrys, today better known as the Spider Orchid, means 'adroitness' and 'skill'. However, all orchids mean 'a beauty' or 'a belle'.

Right: *The Greater Butterfly Orchid* (Platanthera chlorantha). *Butterfly Orchids symbolize 'gaiety' in the flower language.*

Native Species

Left: *The Lady Orchid* (Orchis purpurea) *is a European terrestrial orchid growing in grassland, woodland and scrub.*

The orchid family abounds with plants, having more than 750 genera and at least 20,000 native species - some botanists say more. The range is even wider for cultivated forms, with more than 30,000 hybrids and further ones being introduced each year.

Wild orchids grow throughout most parts of the world. The only continent not represented by them is Antarctica. Some botanists believe the birthplace of orchids to be in Malaysia 100 to 120 million years ago, and their success as plants is clearly evident, since they have adapted to a wide range of climates.

Orchids are prized for their flowers which are specialized, sometimes bizarre and often have intricate parts. They are often brightly-colored and shaped to attract specific insects that will pollinate them.

Orchids are either terrestrial and therefore grow on the ground, or epiphytic and live on the branches of trees. A few orchids live on rocks.

Diversity of Flowers

Above: Brassavola cucullata, *from tropical America.*

Orchid flowers are varied, some solitary and displayed at the tops of stems, others massed in large, lax heads, sometimes pendulous. They all, however, are formed of the same basic parts - the sepals and three petals. Botanically, sepals are a protective layer around the petals - especially when the flower is unopened and still at the bud stage. Collectively they are known as the calyx. Sometimes the sepals are bowl-like, occasionally funneled or tube-like, but usually quite separate and distinctive. It is this variation that helps to create the vast range of differently-shaped flowers. Additionally, orchids are characterized by having one of the three petals modified into a lip.

The flowers are also distinctive because their reproductive parts are formed into a single organ - on many other plants they are quite separate. The pollen bearing male part is just above the ovary, the female element.

Right: Laelia pumila, *a Brazilian species.*

Common Names

Many terrestrial wild orchids have highly descriptive common names, succinctly revealing a plant's appearance. The Lady's Slipper *(Cypripedum calceolus)* has a large lipped yellow petal resembling a lady's slipper. The Stem-less Lady's Slipper *(Cypripedum acaule)* is a close relative from North America, where it is known as the Mocassin Flower.

The Spider Orchids *(Ophrys)* have intimidating flowers resembling spiders, while the Lady's Tresses *(Spiranthes)* reveal flowers that cling to a central stem. *Epipactis repens ophioides* indicates the North American origin of the Rattlesnake Plantain. Its dark bluish olive-green leaves are marked with darker cross veins. The Lizard Orchid *(Himantoglossum hircinum)* reveals a dark hood and a long, strap-like lip, together with an odor of billy goats.

Left: *The Lady's Slipper Orchid*
(Cypripedum calceolus).

Below: Dendrobium aggregatum, *from Burma, Himalayas, Indochina and the Malay Peninsula, has a honey-like scent.*

Color and Scent

Both color and scent play important roles in attracting pollinating insects. Color, of course, is only important during daylight hours, which is why flowers that are pollinated at night by moths are frequently glistening white. They do, however, usually have distinctive shapes that insects can immediately recognize, preventing them wasting time by attending the wrong plants.

Where scent is the main attractant for night-flying insects, it is often only apparent during the hours of darkness and undetectable in daylight. Orchids that do this include *Aerangis* and *Angraecum* from tropical Africa.

Many orchids pollinated during daytime have sweet scents, but some are nauseous and well suited to attract flies. The tropical *Bulbophyllum fletcherianum* has an aroma of rotting meat, while the Lizard Orchid *(Himantoglossum hircinum)* smells like goats.

24

Fragrant Orchids

Cattleya citrina - mellow and sweet, like limes (also known as *Encyclia citrina*)

Cattleya intermedia - musk

Coelogyne barbata - musk

Coelogyne speciosa - musk

Cymbidium simulans - sweet

Dendrobium aggregatum - honey

Dendrobium chrysotoxum - musk

Dendrobium devonianum - musk

Dendrobium moschatum - musk

Lycastes aromatica - lemon

Odontoglossum pendulum - rose

Right: *The Fried Egg Orchid* (Dendrobium chrysotoxum), *from India, China, Thailand and Laos, reveals a musk bouquet.*

Mimicry

As well as using color and scent to attract pollinating insects, some flowers have shapes that mimic insects, encouraging the presence of pollinators that will move from plant to plant of the same species, ensuring pollination and the perpetuation of the species.

The best known mimicry is by orchids that resemble wasps, bees and spiders to attract the right pollinator. Examples of them are found in many orchids throughout the world: the genera *Ophrys* native in North Africa, the Middle East and Europe, and *Cryptostylis* found in parts of Australia.

Evolution has assured that these flowers closely resemble parts of the female pollinator, so that only the male of the species is attracted. The male frequently believes it has found a mate and this is known as pseudocopulation.

Right: *The Broad-leaved Helleborine* (Epipactis helleborine) *is pollinated by a Scorpion Fly.*

26

Orchidmania

Chance played a major role in the introduction of tropical orchids into Europe, creating a mania for orchids that later spread to North America. The first tropical orchid flowered in England as early as 1732 and by the last decade of that century, 15 were growing at the Royal Botanic Gardens, Kew. By 1812, orchids were being grown commercially, but it was not until a consignment of tropical plants was sent to William Cattley of Barnet, north of London, that enthusiasm rapidly grew. The plants he had been sent were, by chance, held together by tropical specimens with strong stems and tough leaves. William Cattley was intrigued by the 'packaging' material and succeeded in rooting some of the stems. In November 1818, these plants produced large, flamboyant flowers that caused a sensation. The plant was named Cattleya.

Left: *This beautiful Cattleya hybrid is growing in the Nani Mau Gardens, Hilo, Hawaii.*

The Mania Spreads

Many orchids collected in the wild were first sent to England, either to botanical gardens or wealthy collectors. Interest in orchids spread and plants were soon being sent to Europe and North America.

Above: Epidendrum fragrans, *native to Mexico, West Indies and South America, bears creamy-white, fragrant flowers.*

Collectors of orchids were mainly in the New England area of North America, and in 1865 a large collection owned by Edward Rand was presented to Harvard University. Today, Harvard is still a major repository of orchids in North America.

One of the earliest nurseries to grow orchids commercially was that of Conrad Loddiges & Sons, Hackney, London, from about 1821. In 1839, it was offering over 1,600 different kinds.

Initially, only the wealthy could afford exotic orchids. Most were expensive to buy and costly to grow, needing high temperatures. It slowly became apparent, however, that many orchids from cooler regions were just as beautiful and could be grown in cooler conditions. About 1850, Joseph Paxton suggested that orchids from cool regions, such as the high altitudes in Mexico, would be ideal for amateur orchid enthusiasts to grow.

Early Collections

The first collection of orchids was started by the Duke of Devonshire in 1833 at Chatsworth House. A man of incredible wealth, he had built a conservatory that covered nearly an acre, and within a decade the largest collection of orchids was amassed. His head gardener, Joseph Paxton, designed and supervised the conservatory's erection, later designing the glass and steel Crystal Palace that housed the Great Exhibition in London in 1851.

The Duke of Devonshire sponsored collectors

Left: *Joseph Paxton (1803-1865), was a gifted gardener and architect, as well as a Member of the British Parliament.*

in their world-wide search for orchids, as well as sending out his own gardener, John Gibson, to India in 1835, returning two years later. Among the orchids he collected were *Coelogyne gardneriana* (now *Neogyna gardneriana*), *Dendrobium devonianum, Dendrobium gibsonii* and *Thunia alba* (now *Thunia bracteata*).

Growing orchids became a status among the wealthy, competing with each other about the size and quality of their collections without any consideration of the costs.

Right: *A truly spectacular orchid –* Dendrobium Brymerianum *– much sought after by early collectors.*

Orchid Hunters

The increasing demand for new and unusual orchids encouraged some orchid growers to turn into professional plant hunters. During the 19th century, many plant hunters searching for new orchid species in Mexico, Central America and tropical regions in South America destroyed whole areas of orchids, both to gain plants and to prevent rival collectors obtaining them. Benedict Roezl (1824-1885) became notorious for the vast numbers he collected: 10,000 plants from Colombia and Panama, a further 3,000 odontoglossums from Colombia, eight tons from Venezuela and ten tons from Mexico, among others. In 1873, he amassed 100,000 plants by agreeing to pay the local natives 10 to 15 francs for every 100 orchids.

Right: Vanda caerulescens *from Burma. A closely related species,* Vanda caerulea, *was collected from the Himalayas 'by the load', but few plants survived.*

First Hybrids

During the 1830s and 1840s, the then world-famous nursery, James Veitch and Son of Exeter, south-west England, sent out plant hunters to many parts of the world. But it was not until Dr John Harris, a physician at a local hospital, suggested a way to successfully cross orchids to John Dominy at the Veitch nursery that man-made hybrids were created.

However, germinating the seeds was still difficult. But in 1922 the plant physiologist, Dr Lewis Knudson, at Cornell University, USA, germinated seeds solely on a mixture of chemicals combined with agar, sugar or glucose and water. The Knudson Formulae has since been used to germinate millions of seeds.

Left: *The introduction of orchids into cultivation inspired painters. Martin Johnson Heade painted this study of hummingbirds and two varieties of orchid in 1882-4.*

Greenhouse Orchids

Greenhouses and conservatories create ideal homes for orchids, but temperatures, humidity, feeding, shading and watering must be tailored to suit individual species' needs.

Because orchids grow in a wide range of climates, the temperatures they need differ dramatically. They can, however, be classified into three types:

Cool: minimum winter night temperature of 7°C/45°F, rising on a summer's night to 14°C/57°F.

Intermediate: minimum winter night temperature of 10°C/50°F, rising on a summer's night to 18°C/64°F.

Warm: minimum winter night temperature of 14°C/57°F, rising on a summer's night to 22°C/72°F.

Some orchid growers recommend slightly higher night temperatures, but avoid day temperatures over 24°C/75°F. Therefore, the greenhouse should be fitted with several

38

ventilators. Electric extractor fans also help to reduce the temperature, removing stagnant air and preventing the occurence of pockets of either cold or very hot air.

Shading formed of roller blinds or hessian helps to prevent excessively high temperatures in summer, as well as reducing the risk of plants being damaged by extra strong sunlight.

Most orchids like a humid atmosphere and this is achieved by mist spraying the plants - but not when in strong and direct sunlight - and dampening the floors and staging. On a summer's day, this needs to be done several times.

Most orchids grow in summer and rest during winter when growth stops. A plant that is about to rest may shed some or all of its leaves, although this depends if it is an evergreen, deciduous or semi-deciduous plant. At this stage, it should be placed in full light and the compost kept dry until new growth appears in spring. Do not mist spray plants during their resting period.

Orchid Care

Several types of composts are needed for orchids, depending on their nature - terrestrial and normally growing in the ground, or epiphytic and supported by trees. Terrestrial types need a compost formed mainly of loam, such as equal parts damp peat, sharp sand, sphagnum moss and fibrous loam. Compost for epiphytic types varies from species to species, but in general a mixture of equal parts of finely-ground bark, sphagnum moss, moist peat and vermiculite is suitable. Specially prepared compost can often be bought ready mixed for both types of orchids and many orchid growers find this very convenient.

Plants are usually bought established in pots. They are repotted in spring, usually every two years, keeping them in small containers. Terrestrial orchids are put into pots, but epiphytic types can also be grown in slatted baskets or on rafts of wood. When potting plants with aerial

Left: *Dendrobium* 'Sailor Boy'.

roots, these should be left outside the container.

When repotting terrestrial orchids, remove the plant from its pot and gently tease away old compost. Replace the plant in a clean pot, trickle fresh compost around the roots, firming it with a small stick. Leave a ½ in (12 mm) space between the compost and rim to enable the plant to be watered.

To repot epiphytic types, remove loose compost and cut away dead roots. Hold the plant upside-down and pack compost around and between the roots, creating a firm ball. Turn this up the right way and place in a container, packing fresh compost firmly around the roots. Do not water the plants for about a week after repotting, then sparingly until the roots are established.

From spring to late summer keep the compost moist - terrestrial types by filling the space between the compost and rim, epiphytic ones by immersing the complete roots in clean water. Orchids can be damaged by excessive feeding.

Below: *When given care and attention, orchids create an array of shapes and color unequaled by other plants.*

$\mathcal{R}$equirements

Duriṅg recent years, orchids have been introduced that can be grown indoors - on windowsills, in sunrooms, with the help of special lights, in cellars and other dark areas that normally would not be suitable for any plant.

Orchids grow in indoor window-boxes, but the aspect must be right. In summer, a position by an east or west-facing window is needed, but in winter, a southerly one is essential so that they have the maximum amount of light. Fill the base of a tray with perlite or other water-retentive aggregate and stand pots of orchids on it. This material must be kept damp, but not awash with water.

Right: *Bathrooms frequently provide the warmth and humidity orchids need, but beware aerosol sprays and wide temperature fluctuations.*

42

Indoor orchids

Brassolaeliocattleya 'Norman's Bay'

Cattleya bowringiana

Coelogyne cristata

Cymbidium devonianum

Cymbidium 'Touchstone'

Dendrobium nobile

Epidendrum cochliatum (also known as

Encyclia cochleata)

Laelia enceps

Maxillaria tenuifolia

Miltonia clowesii

Paphiopedilum callosum

Paphiopedilum fairieanum

Paphiopedilum 'Honey Gorse'

Pleione formosana

Vanda cristata

Starting a Collection

It is essential to buy orchids from reputable sources that will provide you with healthy and strong specimens. A good nursery specializing in orchids will want to sell you high quality plants to encourage your return to buy further specimens.

Before buying any orchid, ask yourself the following questions:

- When fully grown, will there be enough space for it? Never cram your greenhouse full of plants.
- Does its temperature requirements suit the conditions you can provide?
- If it is for growing indoors, will its size eventually mean a move to a greenhouse?

Left: Rhynchostylis retusa, *from tropical Asia.*

Easy-to-grow orchids

Aerides fieldingii
Aerides odoratum
Angraecum eburneum
Bifrenaria harrisoniae
Brassavola nodosa
Bulbophyllum umbellatum
Calanthe masuca
Coelogyne cristata
Coelogyne massangeana
Encyclia mariae
Laelia anceps
Lycastes aromatica
Maxillaria tenuifolia
Miltonia clowesii
Pleione formosana
Rhynchostylis retusa

Right: Coelogyne massangeana, *from Assam, the Malay Peninsula and Java.*

$\mathcal{S}tunningly$ $\mathcal{S}imple$

Orchids are exceptional cut flowers for use in all varieties of floral displays for the home, as well as in decorative accessories for memorable occasions. Not only do they offer a wide color range, but the sprays add a distinctive architectural feature to arrangements, while the individual flowers and buds lend additional visual interest in their unusual and varied compositions.

Orchids are relatively expensive cut flowers to purchase but they are, in fact, good value since they last for several weeks indoors if kept cool and well-watered.

An effective yet simple way to create a bold orchid display is to use a substantial quantity of the same type of orchid Such an arrangement makes a dramatic impact in a modern, minimalist interior. Alternatively, mix just a few stems of a single color orchid with a different type of flower but of the same color.

Simply Red

Dramatic spotlighting brings these flame-red, small-flowered orchids to life against the warm tones of an old oak refectory table.

Use a block or two of florist's foam as a heavy base for the arrangement. Set these on a waterproof base and secure with florist's clay or water-resistant tape for maximum stability. Begin by building a solid center of foliage to conceal the foam blocks. Work all the way round the foam, pushing in the orchid stems. Monitor the shape you are creating as you work - aim for a dense, low arrangement.

Goddess of Light

This exotic table arrangement would make an unforgettable centerpiece for a special reception or dinner party. It is an exercise in subtlety, harmonizing light and shade in combining white Singapore orchids with white roses, variegated foliage and twigs of catkins. The white tapers add interest to the basic equilateral triangular structure, and the flowers positively glow in the light they shed.

Once completed, regularly check orchid arrangements for dying foliage and flowers - the orchids will be the longest-lasting element in the display. Either replenish with fresh material or use the orchids to create a new arrangement.

Fresh and Formal

This luscious pink and green arrangement, designed for a side table, would bring cheer to any traditional interior, set in a handsome bronze cherub container. Several sprays of graceful white Singapore orchids are combined with a deep pink variety, concentrated in the center of the arrangement, together with stems of pink roses and the pink flowering shrub, *Virburnum bodnantense*. Fronds of the bright green fern, *Adiantum pedatum*, and stems of delicate Michaelmas daisy frame the colorful focal point. Touches of darker foliage give depth to the composition.

Golden Garland

To mark the occasion of a Golden Wedding anniversary in sumptuous style, recreate this orchid garland to adorn a wall or door. Alternatively, use different colored bows for a special birthday party or wedding reception.

To make the base, gather together twigs of hazel and intertwine the vines of wild ivy. Build into a circular shape. Using stout wire, attach small terracotta pots firmly to the base. Place a small block of damp florist's foam into the base of each pot. Add tendrils of variegated ivy and sprays of small white and yellow orchids, to trail from the pots. Place one large orchid bloom in the center of each pot. To finish, attach paper or ribbon bows around the garland using a length of wire through the back of the knot.

Bridal Bouquet

Orchids are ideal floral subjects for wedding decorations in that they combine an extravagant appearance with robustness. This elegant bouquet would bring a welcome freshness and color to a winter wedding, whilst avoiding the rather sterile formality of the more common florist's flowers. Here, a couple of sprays of shaded pink Singapore orchids have been combined with several wired orchid flower heads and white spray carnations, to achieve a solid center. The variegated ivy leaves (wired) bring warm tones to the arrangement, and the addition of a few fine stems of Michaelmas daisy and baby's breath *(Gypsophila)* soften the whole effect.

Crowning Glory

Weddings provide a rare opportunity to indulge our romantic fantasies. A fresh flower headdress makes a dramatic bridal accessory, especially when created from exquisite orchids. The design featured here has a fresh, natural quality, using white and lime green Singapore orchids on a base of dark green common ivy with berries. Small sprigs of baby's breath *(Gypsophila)* have been added for highlights and to break up the solidity of the arrangement. The interwoven string of pearls provides a luxurious finishing touch, warmly glowing in the light.

Threatened Species

Like certain birds and animals, many wild plants are becoming rare and on the verge of extinction. Native orchids throughout the world have especially suffered the greed and ignorance of man, since their flowers are attractive and at one time were a status symbol.

Today, no-one should remove the flowers or dig up an orchid growing wild. Many species have been so decimated by having plants pulled up - often only to create a fleeting display in a vase indoors or as part of a pressed plant collection - that they are now about to become extinct.

Right: *The Military Orchid* (Orchis militaris) *is a superb terrestrial orchid that is becoming increasingly rare through plant vandals picking them.*